MY WORLD, MY VIEW

PHOTOGRAPHS
by the girls of SOS Bahini, Pokhara, Nepal

Sue Carpenter

ASHA PUBLICATIONS

in association with the

BRITISH COUNCIL

MY WORLD, MY VIEW

PHOTOGRAPHS

by the girls of SOS Bahini, Pokhara, Nepal

Sue Carpenter

ASHA PUBLICATIONS
Text © 2007 Sue Carpenter, Asha Publications
Photographs © 2007 Sue Carpenter and the girls of SOS Bahini/Asha Publications

First edition

ISBN 99946-2-433-1

ASHA PUBLICATIONS
13 High Street,
Emberton, MK46 5JB
UK
+44 (0) 1234 714089
www.asha-nepal.org
mwmv@asha-nepal.org

in association with the
BRITISH COUNCIL
www.britishcouncil.org

Designed and printed by
PowerComm, Kathmandu, Nepal

Dedication
To the 13 million girls and
women of Nepal,
May they attain equality
where there is inequality,
May they gain power where
they are powerless,
May their views be upheld
where they are disregarded,
May their voices be heard
through the silence

Photo: Devi N

My aunt, Devi,
cooking *sel roti*,
by Sapana

Contents

Sabita28.9.06 145.jpg

Belmaya28.9.06 262.jpg

Sarangkot by Kamala.jpg

Kamala30.9.06 013.jpg

Belmaya30.9.06 062.jpg

Alina22Oct06 bhailo.jpg

Kamala 21Oct06 (28).jpg

Usha4.11.06 013.jpg

Devi T Pagoda.jpg

ParvatiPeacePagoda14Oct06.jpg

SunitaN 24.10.06 (85).jpg

HoliParvati (8).jpg

HoliPramila 195.jpg

Chandra 20.1.07 096.jpg

Nita 21Oct06 (2).jpg

Parvati 24.10.06 067.jpg

Usha4.11.06 023.jpg

SunitaN 24.10.06 (61).jpg

SapanaHome54.jpg

Alina22Oct06 038.jpg

Dr Andrew Hall
His Excellency the British Ambassador to Nepal

I am delighted to introduce this collection of photographs by 22 schoolgirls from SOS Bahini. The aim of the photographic project *My World, My View* was to unlock creativity and self-expression by giving the girls cameras, and encouraging them to develop their own unique vision through the medium of photography. As you will see, the photographs are terrific. The girls, who until recently had never handled a camera before, show a natural feeling for colour and form and composition. And their sheer enjoyment in recording the world around them shines through these pictures.

Girls in Nepal suffer from gender discrimination from birth onwards. Fewer girls than boys survive to reach adulthood. Fewer girls are in full-time education, and literacy rates for women are significantly lower than for men. Employment opportunities for girls are significantly worse than for boys. Women are hugely under-represented in all spheres of public life, including politics. Poverty, social exclusion and poor governance all impact on females to a greater extent than on males. Organisations such as SOS Bahini and Asha-Nepal are helping to protect girls and women from exploitation, to give them a fresh start in life and to empower them. Having had the opportunity to meet many of these children, I have seen for myself how this project has given them a new sense of self-worth and self-confidence.

I sometimes think of the parable of the wise man and his friend who were strolling on the beach when they came across an enormous shoal of fish washed ashore by a storm. Many were still alive. The wise man picked up a gasping fish and threw it far out into the water. Then he picked up another and did the same. Then another. His surprised companion said, "Why are you doing that? There are thousands of fish. What difference can it possibly make?" "Well," said the wise man as he picked up yet another fish and returned it to the water, "it makes a difference to *this* one."

Dr Andrew Hall and his wife Kathie arrive at SOS Bahini, Pokhara, to inaugurate the exhibition of the girls' photos. Photo by Kalpana

My World, My View has made a difference to these young lives and you can enjoy experiencing it through their photographs. Perhaps you too will want to make a difference, by supporting this project so that it can help even more children.

John Fry
Country Manager, British Council Nepal

John Fry with Tommaya, Belmaya, Samjhana and Sapana at the Pokhara exhibition opening, by Kalpana

My World, My View was a project that was so easy to want to support: a British photojournalist teaching photography to disadvantaged girls to give them a means of expressing their present and, hopefully, skills to support their future. It was a project full of optimism and one that spoke directly to the British Council's work in intercultural dialogue.

The initial promise to Sue Carpenter and Asha-Nepal was that we would host an exhibition in Kathmandu at the project's end in June 2007. However, such was the progress of the young photographers, such were the range of excellent images they were producing, that an exhibition was held in February and I suggested this book in March! Why wait till June, when there was already so much palpable achievement?

When Sue's time in Nepal comes to an end, it will not, I hope, be the end of the real project. That will be found in the future of these girls. They are already earning from the proceeds of sales of their photographs. This book will generate more to help secure their livelihoods. What is crucial is that the doors remain open to enable them to find careers in photography if they so wish it, that the skills they have been learning are embellished and exercised rather than atrophy. In turn, they may one day conduct their own *My World, My View* projects for future young photographers.

Finally, my tributes and thanks. First to Sue who is not only an excellent tutor but who is possessed of a refreshing optimism. Her belief and her expertise have made an enduring difference. She was not alone. The staff of SOS Bahini are wonderful and I'm delighted that this book will also support their excellent work. Last but not least to all the girls named and featured in this book, for their engaging openness, their new self-confidence, their charm. Keep your cameras to hand.

Sunita G and Devi N, by Parvati

Peter Bashford
Chairperson, Asha-Nepal, UK

Eight years ago Sue Carpenter and I founded Asha-Nepal with the ambition of combating the trafficking of women and girls from Nepal into the sex industries of India.

Since then we have widened our remit to include women and children who have suffered from physical and sexual abuse, forced labour and other forms of exploitation

and oppression. Even away from the violent extremes, in everyday domestic situations, gender inequality prevails in Nepal. The rights of girls and women are routinely violated throughout their lives.

We work with a small nucleus of seed organisations such as SOS Bahini who are carrying out effective and often groundbreaking projects, to combat trafficking and abuse, and to rehabilitate and empower its victims and potential victims. We have had a real effect on the direction of counter-trafficking activities. However, while the governments of Nepal and India have spoken volubly on the subject, little has been put into practice to end the continued abuse of countless women and children. Those women and children, along with most of their sisters in Nepal, have no voice.

With the photographic project *My World, My View*, an opportunity has opened up for some of these children to speak out and be heard. The 22 girls have gained an insight into both themselves and their world. Their commit-

Peter Bashford with SOS Bahini girls during Holi festival
Photo: Sue Carpenter

ment to the project has created the outstanding body of work that you see in this book. All the participants were in dangerous situations that made them vulnerable to being trafficked, or were actual victims of abuse. They are no longer numbers in a growing set of shameful statistics but human beings with both the confidence and power to share their world with you.

But please remember that behind their glowing work is the painful reality that brought this opportunity about, the real risks that they faced and the dreadful abuse that some of them had to endure. To look at the breadth of emotion portrayed in their photographs, from moments of introspection shown in their portraiture to the enjoyment expressed in their street scenes and the calm of life in their SOS Bahini homes, they give testimony to the resilience of the human spirit and a glimpse into what promises to be a brighter future ahead. This book is a forum for sharing their vision and skills, for telling their stories and for voicing their opinions for the first time.

UNICEF's call for equality...

Gender equality is not only morally right, it is pivotal to human progress and sustainable development. Gender equality will not only empower women to overcome poverty, but also their children, families, communities and countries. Healthy, educated and empowered women have healthy, educated and confident daughters and sons. The amount of influence that women have over decisions in the household has been shown to positively impact the nutrition, health care and education of their children. By upholding women's rights, societies also protect girl children and female adolescents. Without gender equality, it will be impossible to create a world of equality, tolerance and shared responsibility – a world that is fit for children.

... and the UN's call to end violence against females

A 2007 statement by the UN Country Team in Nepal declared that "Violence against women is still a universally tolerated and often unpunished crime... The need of the country is to bring effective laws into practice. The Act on Gender Equality in Nepal has repealed and amended 56 discriminatory legal provisions to ensure women's rights. Now it is the responsibility of all state organs and civil society to join in the efforts to stop violence against women and promote gender justice."

Foreword

Radha Poudel
Chairperson, SOS Bahini, Pokhara

SOS (Save Our Sisters) Bahini, as is very clear from its name, is focused on improving the lives of girls and women in desperate situations. It is heartbreaking to hear the statistics of girls and women suffering the worst forms of assaults in our country: physical and sexual abuse, domestic slavery, drunken husbands and fathers, and, worst of all, trafficking. These issues and our male-dominated society have almost silenced female voices.

In my 27 years of nursing, I travelled all over Nepal and saw many such cases, but then I was very much helpless. Then I met Raymond Lindinger, chairperson of Mettalux, an NGO in Luxembourg. He too felt strongly the need to change the lives of girls and women in Nepal. So in 2004, together we set up SOS Bahini, starting with three children. Today we directly and indirectly look after some 40 beneficiaries.

Gathering children from disadvantaged backgrounds is not difficult in Nepal. What is more important is to give them a better life and make them active in all ways to adjust to society. One such way, in what has clearly

been a turning point in their lives, is their training in the art of photography. This has become instrumental in the lives of our girls, allowing them to take wonderful pictures and more importantly making them realise their creativity.

My World, My View has literally given our girls voices: sharper and louder. There are many things they could never talk about or even think of a way to talk about before. They have today become more expressive through their pictures. I see a lot of photojournalists in the making! Thanks, Sue, on behalf of all my girls. You're an excellent tutor and a great friend to the children.

Today it feels great to have seen two exhibitions of the girls' work, the first one at the British Council in Kathmandu, and the later one at SOS Bahini in Pokhara. The British Council has played a major part in both exhibitions and now in this book, and John Fry has been very supportive throughout. His Excellency the British Ambassador has also been a friend to us, inaugurating both exhibitions and endorsing

this book. Thank you very much, sirs, from all of us at SOS Bahini.

Profits from this book and sales of prints are going into the girls' personal bank accounts and towards setting up a further family home for more girls in desperate need. Thank you so much Asha-Nepal and Sue.

Nepal: the hard facts

- Of a total population of 27 million, over 12 million are under 18, and nearly one million of those are orphans
- 31% of children over 5 are in child labour
- An estimated 12,000 girls each year are trafficked into prostitution in India and domestic slavery in the Middle East
- The average life expectancy is 62. The average life expectancy of girls forced into prostitution is 30
- In a UN Study on Violence Against Children, 2006, of approximately 4,000 children interviewed, 30% had been sexually abused
- The male literacy rate in over-15s is 63%. In females it is 35%
- 73% of females enrol in primary school; 42% enrol in secondary school. These figures don't reflect actual attendance
- 31% of the population are below the poverty line

At the annual picnic: Radha, Surendra, Sue, Simi and the girls of SOS Bahini

Introduction

Sue Carpenter
Project Leader, *My World, My View*

My inspiration for this project came from seeing the documentary film *Born into Brothels*, about children from Calcutta's red light district whose lives were transformed through learning photography. As I read about other similar projects, I saw a common thread – photography could empower the powerless.

I have long been connected with Nepal, from my own journalistic assignments and as a trustee of Asha-Nepal. I know the statistics and I have seen the fall-out: girls in Nepal lie at the bottom of the social heap.

Not only are they discriminated against in very tangible ways – boys may go to school, while their sisters stay at home to work in the house and fields – they also live in a society that expects girls to be submissive and effectively gags them. Girls end up suppressing their feelings and opinions to the extent that they are unable to identify what they feel or think.

Even girls who come from more equal households are let down by the education system in Nepal, which does little to encourage creativity and individuality, valuing instead discipline, conformity and rote-learning.

I wanted to live in Nepal and get directly involved with some of these girls, get to know them, hear their stories and give them a forum to make their own statement in society. The terrible life situations that some of the girls at SOS Bahini have endured could well have led to their being psychologically damaged. Theirs are tales of abandonment, loss, violence and neglect. All are from poor backgrounds; most have lost one or both parents; one was found in rags, barely able to walk or talk. All were leading lives that infringed their rights as a child and limited their potential.

Their resilience, however, is remarkable. While outwardly they may conform, or remain shy of voicing opinions, they have a tremendous underlying vibrancy, joy and humour, which comes bursting to the surface in their personal interactions and through their photographs. I was delighted one day to find one newcomer, fresh

Sue with the girls, by Tommaya

from two years in slave labour, somersaulting down a haystack, shrieking with laughter.

The most important step in these girls' lives, restoring their childhood and sense of self-worth within a loving community, has been achieved by SOS Bahini. I wanted to build on this by encouraging the girls' self-expression and individuality, to develop their self-confidence and help them harness their personal power. The tool was a simple one – a camera with which to document their lives, to capture their reality in all its aspects, in the great tradition of photojournalism.

Simply being in charge of a camera – something that would normally be out of their reach, and certainly not entrusted to a child – immediately made the girls feel good. Nevertheless, at first the girls hung back on the sidelines, taking photos from a safe, polite distance. My mantra became "*najik!*" – close – get close to your subject. As soon as we switched from conventional cameras with fixed wide-angled lenses to digital ones with zoom lenses, the girls became much more bold and direct. The advantage and disadvantage of digital cameras was the massive volume of images – no moment left uncaptured, but thousands to edit!

For Dasain festival in October 2006, those girls who had family members went to visit them taking a camera and one black and white film. Despite our local photo lab developing the films incorrectly (hence the poor quality of some images), these pictures are for me among the most powerful, revealing so much and serving as a prompt for the girls to speak about their former lives. Some of their testimonies are included in this book, anonymously, to allow them to tell their stories openly without fear of recrimination.

I wanted to encourage the girls to see the bigger picture, to examine the inequalities

Sue with Belmaya and Sunita N, by Parvati

and injustices against girls and women in Nepal, and to feel that they could do something personally to effect social change. Many now say they would like to be a photographer, to teach others and to shoot news and human rights stories to make a difference to other children's lives.

At Asha-Nepal, UK, we will be organising international exhibitions and selling this book in order to keep earning for the girls in Nepal. We have made good contacts with the press and photographers of Nepal and my call to them is that they too support their young sisters, nurture their skills, and commission them to do photo stories. As their captivating images in this book show, the girls have not only the talent, but a bold and truly original perspective.

The girls

"When the camera is in my hands, I feel I can take pictures of the world around me with confidence. This will be a memorable moment in my life that I'll look back on. I'd like to be a photographer in the future. I will remember what I've been taught and share the experience with my friends and the next generation"

Kalpana

Sunita G, 11, by Anju

Portraits of the girls, by the girls

The typical portrait in Nepal is a lifeless, formal image. A primary aim in photo classes was to take more candid, natural shots that portrayed the subjects more as they really are. Some of the portraits on the following pages were taken during open photo sessions with no guidance. Others, such as those on this spread, were taken during a portrait workshop, inspired by Anju's captivating shot of Sunita G on the previous page, and Sarita's photo of Alina on page 21. The key was the backdrop, a terracotta wall with reflected sunlight, which lights up the subjects' eyes while avoiding harsh shadows. Of course, a set-up portrait will always be to some extent posed, but the aim was to capture a sense of the subject's character, while paying attention to focus and framing.

Chandra, 16, by Jinita

Devi T, 13, by Pramila

Sabita, 15, by Chandra

Anti-clockwise from top left:
Sisters Usha, 8, by Jinita,
and Sunita N, 13, by Devi T

Anju, 12, by Devi N
Pramila, 12, by Devi N

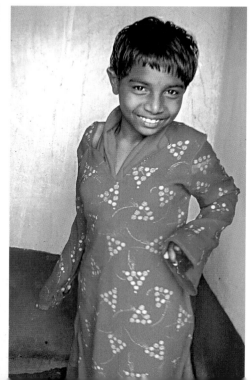

Anti-clockwise from top left:
Sisters Alina, 8, by Sarita,
Laxmi, 10, by Kamala,
and Kamala, 15, by Samjhana,
and their cousin Nita, 9, by Sabita

Sisters Kalpana, 14, *far left*, by Parvati,
Sapana, 11, *below left*, by Devi T,
and Bipana, 9, *right*, by Devi T
This photo: Samjhana, 10, their half-sister,
by Pramila

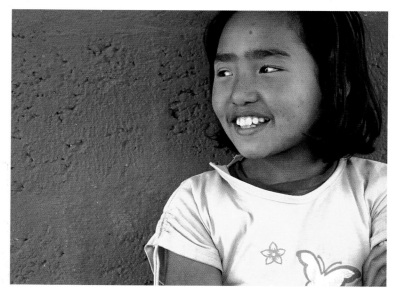

Self-portraits

The girls are fascinated by capturing their own image. Here you can see their experimentation in how they portray themselves (*on opposite page, clockwise from top left*): Tommaya, placing herself firmly in front of the gods at the little temple at SOS Bahini; Kamala, holding the camera purposely upside-down, with henna on her hair; Sarita, looking tentatively into the lens, and Anju's startlingly symbolic picture of a photo of herself behind bars. *This page*: Kamala, *above*, caught in the act by Belmaya, and Anju's photo of her feet – the girls' own feet being another object of fascination.

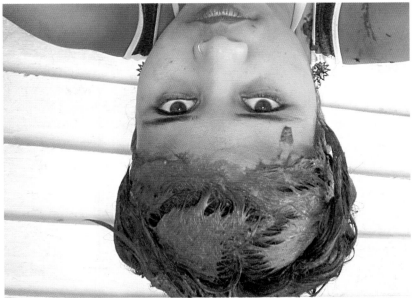

Portraits of the SOS Bahini staff

SOS Bahini has three homes (with two more due to open), each run by a house mother. *Above* is Samjhana's photo of Sharmila, house mother at the main SOS home and day care centre and, *right, from top,* Samjhana's photo of her aunt Dilmaya (natural mother of Kalpana, Sapana and Bipana), Kamala's portrait of her natural mother Krishna (also mother to Laxmi and Alina, and aunt to Nita), and Surendra, administrator of SOS Bahini, captured here on Sarita's first ever film. *Opposite* is Sarita's picture of her mother Meena, who works in the main SOS centre.

"It makes me feel happy and strong having the camera. This photo of my mother was lying on the bed, with the small pictures of my uncle and father at the side, so I just snapped it"

Sarita

Visiting the family home

"Life is hard for women. Men work too, but they don't also have to clean, wash, cook and look after the children. My family lives in the slum area. We have just one room. We wash in the river or bring water to the house. I used to cook and wash clothes for my sisters and brother and I didn't like to go to school. I don't want to get married. I want to be independent and earn my own money. I want to take care of my mother and relieve her from this hard work"

Devi T

My mother and baby brother Sosan, by Devi T

"My *didi*, Saraswati, is older than me but I don't know how old. She goes to school in the village. She's in Class 2, the same as me. I have two *daai*. The younger one is with my father, working in India. This is the older one, Sani. He and his wife and my *didi* live here. I also have a *bhaai* who was four when my mother died. He lives in a childcare organisation in Kathmandu.

My mother had a problem for a long time with her stomach swelling. She was eventually taken to hospital but next day passed away. My father came back from India for the funeral but then went away again.

I like going home, although life is hard. My brother and sister-in-law love me but my *didi* isn't very happy. She wants to live in an organisation like me. She has to cut grass by hand and look after the cows and collect wood from the forest and cook. My brother won't let her go.

He works hard too, ploughing people's fields. We have our own cow and two calfs. We have two rooms, one for cooking, one for sleeping. We cook on an open fire. It's smoky in there. The bed is everyone's. We use the open land as a bathroom. We get water from a public tap.

I'm glad I'm at SOS Bahini. If I was living at home, I wouldn't have a chance to study. I used to go to school but my brother stopped me and said I could go when I was older. He wanted me to work"

Devi N

Devi N's photographs of home during Dasain: My *didi* Saraswati, *left and centre*, and with our *daai* Sani, *right*

"My grandmother doesn't drink or smoke, she likes children's chocolates. She's so kind. If we get sick, she'll take care of us. When we feel hungry we ask her for food and if there isn't any, she gives us money. If a girl is beaten by her stepmother, my grandmother will beat the stepmother.

But not many women are as strong as her. There's a difference between men's and women's rights – men have lots, women's are limited. Men can do any sort of work, they can lie to you, cheat on others, they can do what they like, but women can't. I'd like to photograph women to show the injustices against them – having to cut grass with a knife, collect wood from the forests and carry heavy loads, while men sit and give orders – and if the woman doesn't obey orders, she gets beaten"

Belmaya

Girl working in the field, *above,* by Belmaya
My paternal grandmother, *right,* by Belmaya

34

"This photo was passport-sized, but when my father died we had it enlarged and hung it on the wall. We only have one other photo of him, with my mother. He was kind, he never shouted at us; he used to give us money. Both my parents used to work hard. My father used to leave early in the morning to work for others cutting grass, feeding animals. After he died, they built a highway through our land. Nobody got any compensation.

One night there was a terrible storm. We were in one room and my mother and father were in the other room which was leaking water. My mother was busy trying to throw it out. My father touched the tin roof just as it was struck by lightning. He was thrown to the ground and hit his head on a tin box. My mother was struck too.

We were all crying and frightened. Then the rain stopped and everyone came round. My father had a big cut on his forehead. He died on the way to hospital. My mother lost her hearing in one ear. We had two buffaloes and a goat which died in the storm too. I was small and scared. I just feel sad. I miss him."

Sapana

"I wanted to show Uncle and Auntie in the garden. They are rich and have a lot of land. They grow mustard, rice, wheat, millet, lychees, mangoes, pears and all kinds of fruits. They are kind and love us. Our father and mother used to work for them. Whenever we go there they welcome us and offer us fruit. I love pomegranate the best"

Bipana

"This is our house, where my aunt lives with her son, Santosh. We rebuilt the house after the storm. We felt if we stayed in the same place, lightning would strike twice. The old house was black with smoke. My grandmother is over 86. She's my father's mother. She gives us love and she is kind, but if we touch her belongings she gets angry. She is strong. I don't think I can be like that. I'm scared of people and I'm not so tough"

Kalpana

Kalpana's photographs of home during Dasain:
My grandmother and cousin, Santosh, *above left*
My grandmother and sisters, *above*

"I started working in the fields when I was eight. I had to dig, carry fertiliser, plant maize and remove weeds. I also had to clean the cowshed and the house, take care of my brother's children, cook and bring water from the spring. I went to school for three years, until I was eight, but some days I didn't go. I wasn't good at studying and I couldn't read English, so the teacher used to beat me with a stick.

I am the youngest of six children – I have four brothers and one sister. My father worked ploughing fields. He married many times. My mother was the youngest. I was eight when my father died of TB. He used to drink and smoke a lot. He lay on his bed for months in pain. There are no doctors in the remote villages, only community health workers. Finally he was taken to hospital, but after eight days he came home and died. We didn't realise he was that ill.

A year later my mother died. I was cutting grass when somebody said, 'Somebody has committed suicide'. I rushed home to find a crowd of people and the police, but I wasn't allowed to see my mother. She was already ill – she had lung cancer and used to smoke and drink *raksi*. She was in pain. She used to

dream that my father was asking her to go with him. So she took an axe and chopped her neck.

My mother used to drink far more than my father. She'd shout and beat us with whatever she could find. I was scared of her. My father used to beat her for drinking so much but he

didn't beat us. I loved my father. Life got worse after my parents died. I used to get beaten by my sister-in-law. I was often hungry – we'd eat twice a day, at 9am and 6pm, but nothing in between. We cooked rice and the vegetables we grew – radishes, beans, spinach, chillis – but we didn't have enough *daal*. Almost every day I used to feel I couldn't bear my life.

Once, I asked my brother to wash his own plate, and he said, 'You're the daughter, you're here to wash the dishes.' We started fighting and he caught hold of my hair and threw me out in the yard. My sister and I worked harder than my brothers. Brothers get more time to rest than sisters.

When I was 13, I fell seriously ill, with fever, vomiting, severe headaches and breathing problems. I couldn't climb the stairs, but I still had to work. A social worker came and asked my brother if he would care for me properly or let me go to an organisation. My brother said he'd take care of me, but he didn't. The man came back a week later to see if I'd recovered and I hadn't. He asked again if I wanted to go to an organisation and my brother agreed.

I'm pleased I left. Life is better now in every way – more love, better food, I can walk around freely, go to school, keep clean and have good clothes. But sometimes I still miss my family. I miss my sister.

My dream is to be a photographer. I will study more and more and teach small kids like us. I'd like to stay in the city and rent one room and live there by myself."

Devi T on assignment

"When I first went back to visit, for Dasain, my mother was so surprised to see me and how I'd grown up. Everyone at home was really surprised. Before, I was so different – I was so dirty and now I'm so clean and improved. My mother asked me to stay at home, but I said no, I daren't, because I want to study. So my mother said, study well and be great"

Devi T

Returning home to photograph her family, Devi T is greeted by her younger brother, Ishwar, *left* (photo: Sue Carpenter)

My family, *right*, by Devi T

My grandmother, stepsister Susmita,
mother and brother Ishwar, *left*, by Devi T

My stepsisters Gayatri and Susmita, and
sister Puja, *right*, by Devi T

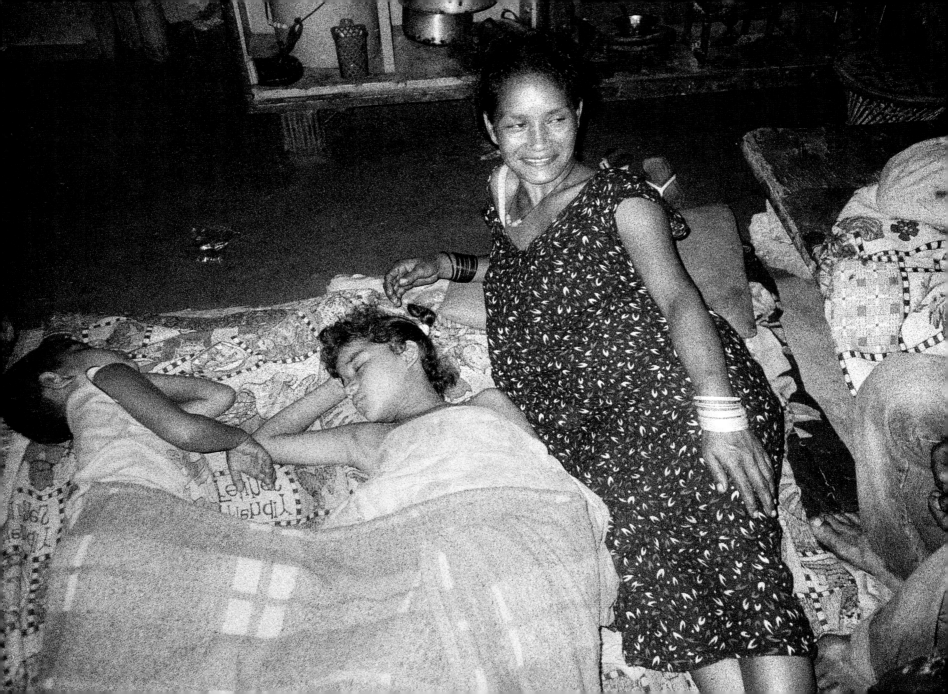

My mother, *bhaai* and *bahini*, *left*
My stepfather, stepsister Susmita and brother Sosan, *below*
My maternal grandparents, *right*
All photos by Devi T, taken during Dasain

- In Nepal, 31% of children over 5 years old are in child labour
- 31% of the population are below the poverty line
- The male literacy rate in over-15s is 63%. In females it is 35%

Left: Puja, helping my mother carrying earth
Right: I used to help my mother selling fruit and vegetables. Now she is a labourer. Here she is, working at a neighbour's house

Photos by Devi T

- 1 out of 3 people in Nepal don't have access to an improved source of water that's safe for drinking (neither at home nor at a community tap)
- 2 out of 3 people don't have access to adequate sanitation and defecate on open ground
- 13,000 children die each year before the age of 5 due to water and sanitation-related diseases and malnutrition

Children with a queue of containers waiting for water at the local tap, *left*, by Devi T
Devi besieged by family and neighbours as she photographs on her street, *below* (photo: Sue Carpenter)
My street, *right*, by Devi T

At our SOS Bahini homes

"I feel lucky to be here. I feel safe and cared for. We have a very nice auntie, Sharmila, who loves us very much, and Mommy, Radha, gives us lots of love and Sue *didi* loves us very much too and we have our uncle who interprets. I never had the opportunity to go to school before, but now I can study so that I can get a job. I have better food and a good place to sleep "

Pramila

Dilmaya cooking, by Sabita

On these and the following pages, the girls capture each other going about the activities of the day – getting ready for school, cooking, eating, studying, helping with chores, playing. In photojournalism, the aim is to tell a story in pictures, to show the truth by shooting every aspect of the subjects' world. Spending all their time together and knowing each other intimately, the girls were able to capture moments and nuances that an outsider may have missed.

This section shows how the girls picked up some key points of photography tuition:

najik ("close" – initially an alien concept but now the girls love getting close to their subject, often shooting still lifes or photos of existing images, such as posters or the TV)

light (although there's no stopping the girls shooting throughout the day, the scenes here in the early morning light – Sabita's on the previous page and Sunita N's, right, both reminiscent of the Dutch artist Vermeer – show how some are using light to add texture and mood to a scene)

natural (more and more, the girls capture life and people in an uncontrived way)

But how to take a truly great image can not be taught. It occurs through instinct and a good eye. A great image has the power to move the viewer and keep drawing him back to look more deeply. It often has a stillness amid the turmoil. Some of the girls' photos have just that.

Getting ready for school: Kalpana, *far left*, by Devi T; Sunita G, *left*, by Tommaya; Dilmaya doing Sapana's hair, *right*, by Sunita N

"When books and pens are in my hands I have to study, but when I have the camera in my hands I can have fun taking photos. I never feel bored with the camera.

Boys say, this is a girl, she can't do anything, but I want to make money and lead my life independently and show them I can do something. I'd like to be a photographer. If I take good photos I can sell them"

Belmaya

Sharmila arranging plates, *below left*, by Devi T,
Sunita N and Devi N, enjoying *daal bhat, below,* by Parvati
Belmaya, *right*, by Sunita N

"Sunita had just stolen someone's Chocofun and was taken to the office and told off. She came back and cried. She was new here, she didn't understand. She was sitting, playing with her book. I wanted to show how she was feeling after doing something wrong"

Kalpana

Left from top:
Chocopies, by Devi T
Hibiscus, by Nita
Gods on the dining room wall, by Bipana
Right:
Sunita G, by Kalpana

From left to right:
Kitchen block at SOS Bahini day care centre, by Chandra
Meena and Belmaya cutting straw for Uma and Dolly the
cows, by Pramila
Meena and Uma, by Sarita
SOS Bahini day care centre, by Sunita G

Testimony: the domestic slave

"My father used to love me very much when I was little, and my mother too. I come from a village in Sindhupalchowk district. I'm the second of five sisters. I never went to school. I worked in six different places before coming to SOS Bahini. I started aged ten. One day my father and mother told me that everyone's daughter works: go and work instead of doing nothing at home.

My father took me to Kathmandu to a house where my mother's sister was working. I didn't know what to do at first. I missed my parents. I cried at night. I slept with my aunt but she didn't comfort me.

I had to wash the *puja* place, clean the gas cylinder, the floor and windows, wash clothes. We used to wake up at 3am and go to bed at 9pm, there was so much work to do. I didn't earn anything. My father just sent me there because he couldn't afford to look after me. I was shouted at and accused of not working properly, so one day I asked the owner's wife for bus money and I went home.

After that I went to another place where my *didi* was working. We didn't earn any money there either. One day I had gone to buy vegetables and when I came back my *didi* was crying. The house owner had beaten her with a belt, accusing her of losing his socks. So we ran home. My parents were happy to see us. They asked how it was but I lied and said everything was fine. I didn't want to make them unhappy. After a month a neighbour found me more work. I realised my parents didn't have enough to eat so I had to help.

I had to cut grass by hand, graze the cows and goats and help an old lady. I still didn't earn money. After that I worked in a restaurant, washing dishes, and then a house where I had to look after a small baby and wash her clothes. Finally an uncle took me to Pokhara to work for another family member who ran a momo and chowmein restaurant.

I had to clean the toilets and bathroom, wash the dishes, clean tables and wash the baby's clothes. The owners used to bathe in their own

bathroom but I had to use the canal. The owner's wife used to beat me all over. Sometimes she'd hide things and blame me for losing or stealing them. My wrists started swelling and my hands were raw from washing and scrubbing.

One day, a Western woman and Nepali man came in and saw my wrists. They told me they'd take me to a clinic. The owner's wife said, 'They might sell you.' I said, 'I don't care.' It couldn't be worse. But they did take me to the clinic and I stayed there several weeks while I was treated.

I never went back to work. I am now at SOS Bahini, where I've learnt to read and write in three months and I'm about to start school with the other girls. My wrists have not fully recovered. I still have to have injections every 21 days at the hospital.

I haven't seen my *didi* since we worked together. She's working in a dance restaurant in Kathmandu. I found out she had visited home and so I phoned her. She said, 'Who are you?' I said, 'It's me, your sister,' and she said, 'No, my sister's already dead.' I don't know why. She didn't want to talk to me. She put the phone down.

My *bahini* is working washing dishes in Kathmandu now. I wish she could come and live here. Life isn't hard any more. At the restaurant I had to sleep on the stairs, at the turning where there's more space. I wouldn't be scared to go back and photograph the owner and his wife – I want to show them I have a better life."

The Rights of the Child

The UN Convention on the Rights of the Child was created in 1989 to make sure that the world recognised that children have human rights. These are: the right to survival; to develop to the fullest; to protection from harmful influences, abuse and exploitation; and to participate fully in family, cultural and social life. The four core principles of the Convention are non-discrimination; devotion to the best interests of the child; the right to life, survival and development; and respect for the views of the child.

Signatories must prevent the abduction or trafficking of children and their economic exploitation, and protect the child from all forms of sexual exploitation and sexual abuse. They must ensure that children under 18 do not take a direct part in hostilities, and uphold the right of the child to an education that develops the child's personality, talents and mental and physical abilities.

Children are entitled to the freedom to express opinions and to have a say in matters affecting their social, economic, religious, cultural and political life. Participation rights include the right to express opinions and be heard.

Nepal signed and ratified the Convention in 1990 – before King Gyanendra took over and the Maoists took a stranglehold on the country. Nevertheless, the nation has flouted the Convention on all the above counts. With much talk since the April 2006 Uprising of a "New Nepal" and the hope of a true democracy, will the new elected government ensure that children's rights are, at last, made a priority?

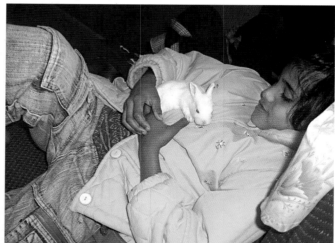

Sapana dancing on the rooftop, *left*, by Samjhana
Anju at Dasain, *top*, by Alina
Alina with baby rabbit, *above*, by Laxmi
Girls enjoying the Dasain *ping* (swing), *right*, by Usha

"I've learnt more about my own world, I'm looking more. Before I didn't know anything but now I've learnt how to take photos and frame them properly. It makes me feel more confident having the camera in my hands. I want to take pictures of everything. At first I took pictures of things like the cow, rabbits, friends, but now I'm taking pictures of activities like cooking, washing, changing clothes, boating, people at the temple. I like getting close up"

Parvati

The trouble with igniting the girls' passion for photography is that there is no escape from the paparazzi. For Holi, the Festival of Colours (and water and eggs, I discovered), Peter Bashford and I went along brandishing cameras, determined to stay clean and dry. No such luck – we were instant targets.

Sue

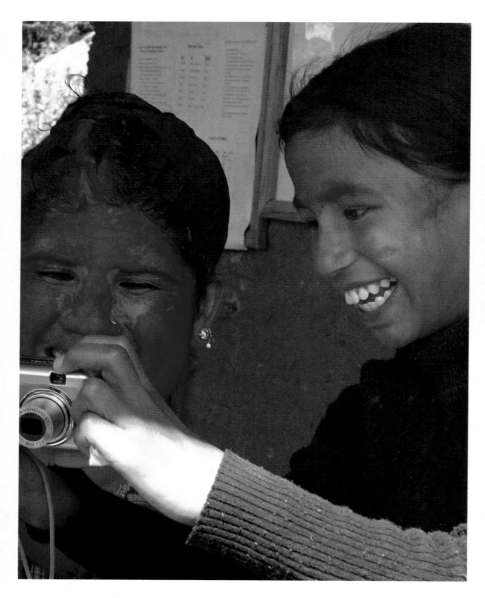

Pramila shows Sharmila her photo, *left,* by Devi T
Samjhana, new arrival to SOS Bahini, and Tommaya, *below,* by Pramila

"I love taking photographs because it's fun and it shows my environment. When we grow up we can be professional like Sue and show our parents what we can do – my parents will be proud of me"

Pramila

"The hardest thing about my old life was that my father and mother always used to fight. Baba is a taxi driver and when he gets paid he drinks. He used to get drunk and beat my mother and we children would hit him with a broom or bite him or pull his hair to stop him. He only beat me once – he picked me up by my hair and threw me on the floor.

When I was 12 my friend and I ran away to live on the streets. At first I said no, but she was my best friend since childhood and I always went along with what she said. We spent a year there. We'd go to the bus park and beg. We'd pretend we couldn't speak. We could earn 100 rupees a day, and we'd buy food and go and see movies. Other times we couldn't get anything so we wouldn't eat.

We slept on rice sacks. It was dangerous. Some people would shout at us, and a street boy used to throw stones at us. If somebody came near, we'd always run away. Thinking about it makes me feel unhappy. I was so sad and hopeless. We were filthy and people used to tease me that I was a white person because my hair was grey with dust.

I wanted to go home but I was afraid my mother would beat me if I went back. Finally we were picked up by an organisation and brought to SOS Bahini. After a few days we tried to escape to freedom but somebody saw us. My friend was sent back to the other organisation, and after she'd gone I settled down here. At first I didn't like the schedule and rules, but two older girls convinced me I should take this opportunity to study. Now I feel stupid for having run away. The worst time of my life was begging on the streets. Now is the best time."

At school

"I went to school before, but sometimes I used to go with my mother to help in the fields or wash plates in other people's homes. This school is much better. I used to get beaten at my last one, but I don't get beaten here. I didn't have enough pens and paper before. Now I do. I like to study and play. I am in Class 2. I'd like to finish Class 10 and go to college and work and earn lots of money"

Sunita G

My class, which has 66 students, by Devi T

"Miss was leaving school on her motorbike. In class she has to be strict, but here she's so happy. I wanted to show her at this moment when she's so different"

Kalpana

74

My feet, *left*, by Belmaya
Schoolfriend, *right*, by Parvati

"I took this picture of the samosas in the school canteen, waiting to be cooked. They're delicious but my favourite food at school is pineapple biscuits"

Sarita

Clockwise from top left:
Schoolfriend, by Kamala
Samosas, Sick bay, School bus, all by Sarita
Right:
Girls at Motherland school, Pokhara, by Laxmi

A trip to Sarangkot

"**E**verybody was very excited to go on our first field trip to the hilltop viewpoint at Sarangkot. It was 4.30 am and we were all singing as we drove by bus to the foot of the hill. I can't believe these mountains we have in our country. I hadn't seen them in the morning before from Sarangkot. They make me forget everything and feel very happy"

Kamala

The view from Sarangkot, by Kamala

Old man, *left*, by Chandra
Goats being herded down to market for Dasain,
above, by Belmaya
Sunrise from Sarangkot, *right*, by Belmaya

"The police at the top of Sarangkot were playing carrom. I was scared to take their photo, so I did a close up of the carrom board and counters. I liked the design they made.

If I take a photo and my brother also takes one and his is better than mine, I know that next time I can take one as good as his or even better. I feel that confidence that if I can't do it today I can do it tomorrow"

Belmaya

Temple bowl, *left*, by Sabita
Carrom board, *right*, by Belmaya

Dasain at Bindyabasini Temple

"It was Maha Astami, the sacrifice day of Dasain. Many people had come to do *puja* and sacrifice the animals. If I had gone without the camera I'd just go and come back, but this made me look more closely. Before I'd done the course, I would stand far away. But after photo training, I go close. I was trying to show exactly what people were doing. One man was breaking a coconut, and another woman was selling coconuts, sweets, flowers and *prasad*. There were many goats in line waiting to have their throats cut. If we give some blood to Durga, the destroyer of evil, it will keep her happy"

Kamala

Boy captivated by burning incense, by Laxmi

From left to right:
Women queuing to worship Durga,
Bindyabasini temple, and Sadhu with tiger's head,
all by Usha

Incense sticks, *this page top right*, by Belmaya
All other photos by Kamala

"I went down to where they were sacrificing the goats and saw lots of blood. I felt scared. But it is good to kill animals for the gods. The gods are good and we should always offer water and *prasad* and worship them to keep them happy"

Sapana

Goats to the slaughter:
by Kamala, *left*, and Sapana, *centre* and *right*

Tihar, Festival of Lights

"Tihar is my favourite festival. I love to dance for *bhailo*. Then we have Laxmi Puja, which means we'll be rich. Everyone lights up their houses with candles to guide Laxmi, the goddess of wealth, to their homes. The next day is Bhaai Tika, when we give *tika* to our brother and he gives us presents and money. It's the day he honours his sisters. We don't have brothers but we have a cousin and we have Raymond Daddy"

Laxmi

Tika tray, by Sunita N

"We spend many days practising for *bhailo,* when we go to each other's homes and sing a song or dance, and they give us sweets, money and flowers. We sing about love, or our mothers, or our country"

Laxmi

Practicing a dance routine, *left*, by Usha
Final rehearsal for *bhailo*, *right*, by Alina

" We make the footprint of Laxmi with flour and water, with red *tika* toes, so she can find her way to the room where we make *puja*. When I see that footprint, I think, ooh, Laxmi Puja – we eat apple, dates, popcorn, banana and chocolate. That's what I like best"

Parvati

Clockwise from top left:
Making footprints, by Usha; Footprint, by Parvati
Puja offerings, and Candles to lead the way, both by Kamala
Right: Radha and Meena give *tika* to Raymond, by Sarita

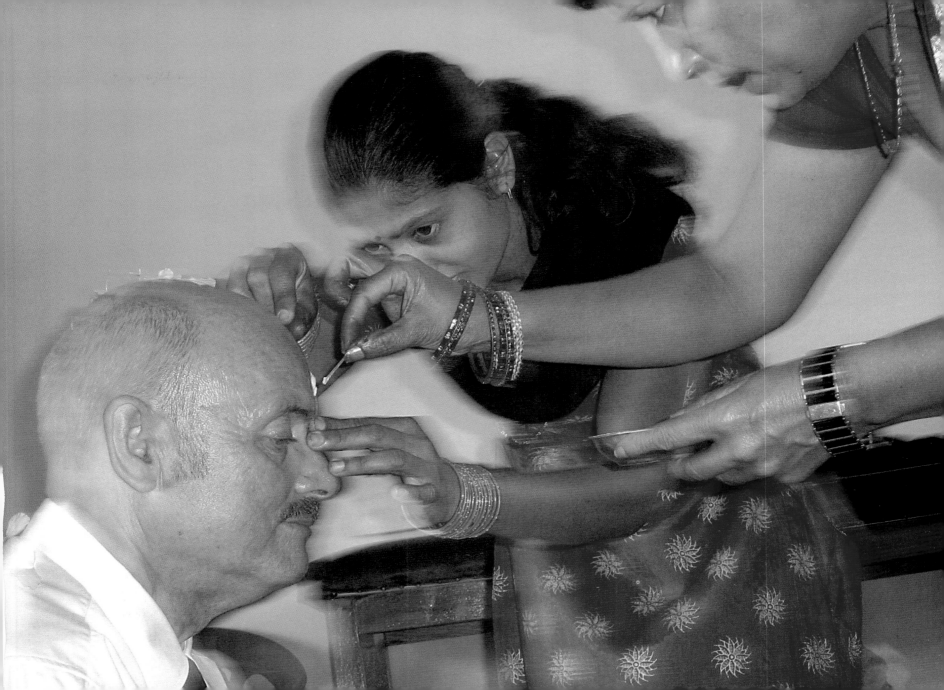

Left to right:
Meena with bangles, by Sunita N
Girls receiving *tika*, by Sunita N
Kalpana, Devi T and Belmaya dancing, by Bipana

A trip to the World Peace Pagoda

One day we took a boat trip across Phewa Lake and climbed up to the World Peace Pagoda, a Buddhist stupa that forms a classic landmark on the skyline of Pokhara. As it was the tail end of the rainy season, the mountain view was obscured by clouds and we were plagued by leeches. The photographic opportunities didn't look promising. However, the girls zoomed in with their lenses and came back with some of their best shots

Sue

World Peace Pagoda, by Devi T

Rice paddies, *left*, and Buddha,
right, both by Sunita N

"This is my favourite picture. I was photographing the money and thinking of all the things I could buy if I had that money"

Parvati

Donation box at Tal Barahi Temple on the island in Phewa Lake, *left*, and tourist at World Peace Pagoda, *right*, both by Parvati

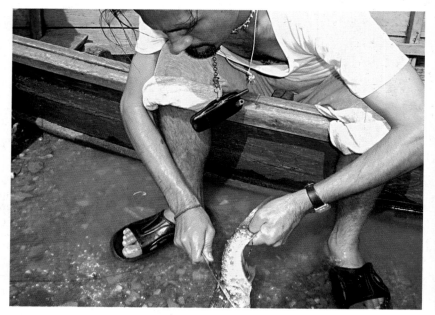

"While we were waiting for the boatman to come I was busy photographing. The man looked like a ghost with his beard, but I was interested in the knife and the fish. Anju was sitting in the boat, hungry and bored, wondering when we would get home"

Parvati

Belmaya Ktm7 02.07.jpg

Belmaya Ktm15 02.07.jpg

Devi T Ktm8 02.07.jpg

Devi T Ktm13 02.07.jpg

Devi T Ktm14 02.07.jpg

Devi T Ktm15 02.07.jpg

Devi T Ktm19 02.07.jpg

Devi T Ktm20 02.07.jpg

Devi T Ktm24 02.07.jpg

Devi T Ktm28 02.07.jpg

Devi T Ktm29 02.07.jpg

Parvati Ktm12 02.07.jpg

Parvati Ktm33 02.07.jpg

Parvati Ktm51 02.07.jpg

Parvati Ktm54 02.07.jpg

Parvati Ktm59 02.07.jpg

Parvati Ktm101 02.07.jpg

Parvati Ktm103 02.07.jpg

Parvati Ktm109 02.07.jpg

Parvati Ktm141 02.07.jpg

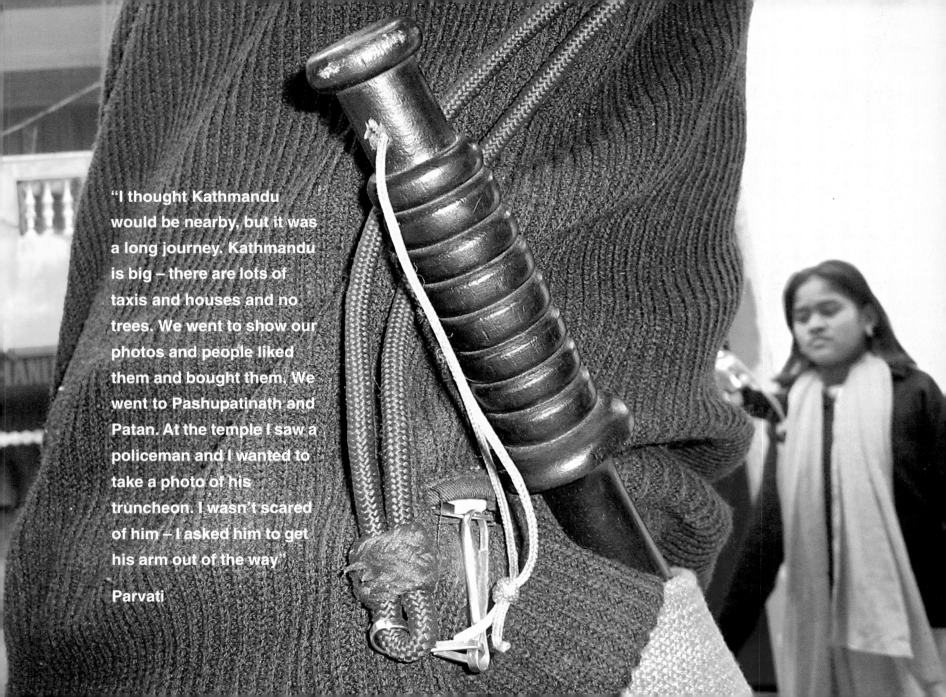

"I thought Kathmandu would be nearby, but it was a long journey. Kathmandu is big – there are lots of taxis and houses and no trees. We went to show our photos and people liked them and bought them. We went to Pashupatinath and Patan. At the temple I saw a policeman and I wanted to take a photo of his truncheon. I wasn't scared of him – I asked him to get his arm out of the way"

Parvati

Acknowledgments

This book, along with the exhibitions in Nepal and future ones to be held internationally, are important outcomes of the *My World, My View* project, to validate and showcase the girls' talents and worth, and to earn revenue for the girls and their organisation. To all those who contributed time, money and support towards making the book and exhibitions happen, very many thanks.

Special thanks

To all those people who had faith in the project from the outset and helped fund my journey and the equipment – particularly to Mehra Dalton of Greaves Travel, Sunetra Atkinson, Robin and Charlotte Fry, Will Bowen, Indigo Trading, Barty Smith, Anna Cryer, Arthur Lyons, Chris Patterson, Anna Lempriere and Rosemead School.

To Kodak, PhotoVoice and those individuals who donated cameras and film.

To Peter Bashford of Asha-Nepal, for all his support and his tireless work for girls and women in Nepal; to Raymond Lindinger, of Mettalux, and Radha Poudel and Surendra Pariyar of SOS Bahini for opening their doors so generously to me and Simi, and for having faith in the project; to Douglas Maclagan and all at Child Welfare Scheme for their part in getting me to Nepal and support on the ground in Pokhara.

To John Fry at the British Council, Nepal, for supporting *My World, My View* from the start, for so generously hosting and sponsoring the exhibition in Kathmandu, and, above all, for sponsoring this book. A book was the outcome we hoped for and dreamed of; John made it a reality.

To His Excellency the British Ambassador Dr Andrew Hall and his wife Kathie Hall, for their ongoing support and warm interest in the project and its beneficiaries.

To Tek Suhang, my interpreter and long-suffering assistant, who became friend and "uncle" to the girls, and is now in Britain studying for an MBA.

To Will Bowen and Chris Burke, who helped me via cyberspace to design the exhibitions and accompanying posters and flyers. To Paulette Disher and Hanneke Blum for moral support and helping mount the exhibition in Kathmandu. To Prajwal Shrestha at PowerComm for the great design of this book.

To all those, too numerous to mention, who have bought prints or made donations in Nepal, raising so far in excess of 40,000 rupees for the girls' personal savings accounts, a big thank you from all of us.

And finally to all the gorgeous girls of SOS Bahini, whose warmth, passion, mischief and laughter will remain in my heart and beaming from my walls.

Sue Carpenter

With thanks to the United Nations and UNICEF for permitting us to quote from the following documents, which can be viewed online:

The State of the World's Children, 2007
www.unicef.org

The Convention on the Rights of the Child
www.ohchr.org/english/law/crc.htm

Asha-Nepal is a human rights organisation working for women and children in Nepal, primarily concerned with the rescue and rehabilitation of trafficked women and girls and their reintegration into society. Founded in 1999, it funds a family unit with a house mother at SOS Bahini, as well as refuges, vocational training schemes, self-help groups, support for those who have contracted HIV while in abusive situations, and other rehabilitation and self-sufficiency projects.

British-registered charity no 1082581

Asha-Nepal,
13 High Street,
Emberton, MK46 5JB
UK
+44 (0) 1234 714089
www.asha-nepal.org
admin@asha-nepal.org

SOS Bahini (SOS stands for "Save Our Sisters", and *bahini* means "little sister") is a Nepali-run NGO, with a board of 10 women, who believe that caring for children in a family environment is more effective than an institutional approach. They look after girls who have come from desperate situations (sexually and/or physically abused, orphaned, in forced labour, homeless, suffering from the effects of severe poverty, at risk of being trafficked). Girls live in homes with a house mother, and are given nutritious food (with home-grown vegetables and fresh milk and eggs from their own cows and chickens), education, counselling and awareness programmes, healthcare and vocational training.

SOS Bahini
PO Box 331
School Patan,
Lakeside, Pokhara 06,
Kaski, Nepal
+977 (0) 61 551942
sosbahini@gmail.com

The **British Council** is the world's leading agency for cultural relations. It builds mutually beneficial relationships between people in the UK and other countries, and increases appreciation of the UK's creative ideas and achievements. It gives people in other countries access to learning opportunities and creative ideas from the UK, as well as making opportunities for UK citizens to make contact with, and learn from, people, ideas and expertise in other countries.

www.britishcouncil.org

Glossary	
Didi	older sister
Bahini	younger sister
Daai	older brother
Bhaai	younger brother
Ba, baba	father
Puja	worship/offering/blessing
Prasad	food offering to gods
Tika	celebratory/religious coloured daub on forehead
Daal bhat	Nepali staple diet - lentils, rice, vegetable curry
Sel roti	Fried rice flour doughnut rings, eaten at celebrations

Anju, by Kalpana, *overleaf*